TAKE
OVER
TUES
DAY

55 Inspiring Short Stories to Help You Win in Business & Life

TONY ROUSE

ISBN: 0692672206
ISBN-13: 978-0692672204

DEDICATION

This book is dedicated to a group of guys that allowed me to bombard their email week after week in an attempt to just share what I knew that while in the process would grow us all. Thank You, Gentlemen.

The Firestarters:
Booth Armstrong · Shane Bonilla · Mitchell Brown
Aaron Corn · Will Fogleman · Rob Fogleman · Keith French
Dean Fung-A-Wing · Gabe Fung-A-Wing
Mike Fung-A-Wing · Quinn Fung-A-Wing
Jonathan Goldin · Jay Greiner · Wes Hendrix · Chris Hylton
Justin Norwood · Chris Patton · Matt Reibling · Ben Rouse
Chris Sherry · Cy Whitfield · Kevin Zhang

TAKEOVER TUESDAY

CONTENTS

TAKEOVER TUESDAY

ACKNOWLEDGMENTS

I'd like to acknowledge my family, who have always been there for me with voluntary and involuntary support... I'd like to thank all of my friends for a continuous understanding of 'My Next Great Idea'. And lastly, I appreciate all of my mentors for talking me off the ledge when I needed it and at times pushing me over it because I wouldn't have gone otherwise...

TAKEOVER TUESDAY

INTRODUCTION

What started as a text message amongst a group of guys in early 2013 has now turned into an internationally shared platform of motivation and success by people from all walks of life.

As a part of its platform, Takeover Tuesday has successfully featured doctors, pastors, entrepreneurs and everything else in between in the exposition of greatness and many people have asked, 'Tony, Why Tuesday?!?' and my response was simply that it just sounds the best for who we are and what we do.

Not knocking any other clever quip involving a day of the week, but I personally got to a point in my life where I was simply not satisfied with barely making it... I was looking to conquer in all that I went to do... I was in place to 'Takeover'. That meant literally taking control of all aspects of my life as they related to everything I was involved with.

And with that said... I am excited to present to you a collection short stories written to help you win in business and life. It is my sincere hope that these stories speak to you and that you find points of connection throughout the 55 entries we have included that will fuel your fire for success and ignite your passion to win in all that you go to do.

"There is no reason to be beat up when you have been given the power to Takeover."

- Tony Rouse

WHAT ABOUT PINOCCHIO?!?

Remember the beloved tale of Walt Disney's Pinocchio? You know the one about a carpenter named Geppetto, that built a marionette puppet that became a boy... Yeah, that one. Something hit me that I just want to expound upon. In the very beginning of the movie way before Pinocchio had the issue of lying and his nose growing was that Geppetto made a wish. The wish was to have the puppet become a real boy. Now minus all the fairy dust and stuff... I thought the most interesting part was that Geppetto had a wish or a dream for something he had already built.

Stay with me...

Many times we all have a wish or a dream, but we do nothing to act upon it. We have nothing in place that can be acted upon to get something done. Case in point... you want to be an author, but you haven't written a book. You have a grand scheme, but nothing in place that is tangible to move you forward in any direction. If nothing else (this my own interpretation) Geppetto built a replica and had an expectation of a miracle. At least he had a model, scale or structure of something he was after.

Stop.

Take an assessment of your dreams, visions and goals and go build something. Have something that is in the process that it can be taken to the next level. How can we have an expectation of greatness when we haven't done anything to rightfully propel us towards it?

Watch Me Get Deep on Disney...

THE POWER OF THANK YOU...

I cannot begin to express in words the joy that I have at this current moment. Not the fact that I'm excited about my own life, but really that of others. I'm starting to see breakthroughs happen for other people and that has me pumped up for their next level of success. It's interesting that my thankfulness is in the form of other people's successes because I'm excited to see them win. I remember at one point about a year ago when I was lost and confused a bit. I felt abandoned, alone and afraid. I remember crying out to God for a why am I here... why me mindset. But at some point I flipped the switch and just said: "I'm not dead... What needs to happen from this point to get me to the next one... And how exactly are we going to do that?" I realized that this problem/situation was not only my exit strategy from failure, but most importantly my entrance exam into greatness.

I started recognizing the little victories and the everyday occurrences that we all seem to take for granted. I became happy in the fact that there was breath in my lungs and life in my veins. As cheesy as it may sound, I was like Leonardo DiCaprio's character of Jack in Titanic. *(Side Note: I didn't like this movie that much... I remember just waiting for the boat to sink...and I also think I would have found a board, dining room table or something to survive on at the end. I'm just saying...)* ...But I was thankful! I changed my mindset from victim to victor and pursued greatness at all costs. It was important for me to win. Was I exactly where I saw myself with my vision?!? No... BUT I was not where I was! I realized I had moved from that place of mediocrity and inferiority and traveled further down the road to the place and palace that fueled my dreams. And all along the way I was and still am **THANKFUL**.

I'm thankful for this platform that I have to share stories of achievement with all of you. I'm grateful for my life and how I get the opportunity to live it and share it with others. I appreciate the transformations that are happening to people all around me and I most excited about the journey and road ahead.

I dare you... Be Thankful.

I challenge you to say Thank You. Not only will it revolutionize your external relationships, but it will radically redefine your internal ones. The power that is held in the words, "Thank You" says that I'm acknowledging that "you" helped me when I needed it most and for that I am so grateful.

FEAR...

Fear...Is it holding you back? So many times we are reluctant to act out on our dreams because we are scared that everything is going to go horribly awry. But, what if it doesn't and you were completely wrong in your analysis of that situation. The suggestion is to not throw caution to the wind, but a literal definition of insanity is expecting different results while doing the same thing.

You can't expect to reach a goal if you never take a step towards it. When you start to operate in Fear you shut off your mechanism to walk in Faith. So to go from Fear to Faith... Flip It. Flip Fear and the only other option you have is Faith. Many of us are very connected to pessimistic ideals that when optimism is presented it is seen as something that is so unattainable it is not a reality. The funny thing about life is that there are really only 2 choices: Acceptance or Rejection. You are either going to do one or the other. If you don't make a choice, Rejection is automatically made for you. So accept your dreams and take a step to live... or reject them and stay exactly where you are.

"It is not death that a man should fear, but he should fear never beginning to live."

- Marcus Aurelius

MINIMUM RAGE...

Are you guilty of being the definition of average... best of the worst / worst of the best? Are you picked last during all of your office parties? Does your life suck and you want to do something radically different??? (Yeah I know this sounds like the intro to a bad infomercial from the '90s, but I'm making a point...)

Late last year I began exploring a topic I dubbed, "The Assassination of Mediocrity". It was a pivotal self-reflective moment where I asked myself if I was doing all that I could to be great. I was determined to eliminate basic living in every aspect of my life. 'Ho Hum' was not a lifestyle that I was ready to enjoy.

This past week I had the opportunity to make a presentation and to be frank, there were no additional requirements outside of showing up... but I wanted to do something different. I was determined to deliver a customized Tony Rouse experience. What was different was that I made a fully interactive engagement that chronicled amazing possibilities. Was it necessary? No. Was it memorable? Absolutely. When you go the extra mile you say to yourself and those around you that 1.) I respect you 2.) you will get nothing but the best from me.

The French have a word called 'Lagniappe' which basically means a little something extra. Many have referenced this in the pastry world as a baker's dozen. Meaning you paid for 12, but I'll give you 13 just because I like you and I'm feeling generous. What is so interesting about this concept is that it allows individuals to freely give. Not only are the recipients excited, but it also puts the giver in the position of generosity in doing for others unexpectedly.

When I say 'Minimum Rage', I look at it as a lifestyle adjustment wherein that I don't want anything that is average around me. On a personal note, I should never be someone who does just enough. I'm not comfortable being comfortable... that is not excellence and will not lead to great things. I love the quote that says, "You will never reach millionaire status with a minimum wage work ethic." And I'll tell you firsthand, if you want to be great... serve great.

SEE IT, BEFORE YOU SEE IT...

Over the weekend I pulled out a vision board that I had began some time ago that I didn't complete and it made me think about the fact that why was this even important. Did it really matter that I put my thoughts and dreams on some large scale poster board? Did it really mean anything to cut up my magazines and position "my life" in front of me? Then I thought well yeah… it actually does. I remember a few years ago I had a game plan to create a world of excitement and engagement that I could welcome people in to. And it all started in my notebook. What became 'The Food Rave' was actually many thoughts on a piece of paper. I designed it from top to bottom with all the intricate details, the color and the feel and vibe. I lived and breathed what I saw in my mind. Of course it went on to win Best Social Event from the International Special Events Society and also garnered a nomination for Atlanta Marketer of the Year - Best in Event Marketing. (I must say I had an amazing team that I worked with on that project.)

But the point of this conversation is to bring those thoughts and inanimate ideas in your mind to reality. "You have to see it, before you see it, or you're never going to see it!" is one of the best phrases I ever heard because it makes you realize that if you desire something… you can have it, but it is your responsibility to make it happen. Yesterday was the celebration of Dr. Martin Luther King, Jr. and many recognize his world renowned oratory called, "I Have a Dream." And in that same vein, I say "Don't Stop with a Dream!" Get a plan then get a goal. The life that you really want is already constructed in your mind... you just have to be willing to bring your concept to reality. To do this sometimes it takes a lot of quiet time and I fully understand it may be hard, but if it's worth it... make it happen. I'll tell you it's not the most fun experience of all of the time, but that 4 a.m. wake-up is worth it if you want to life far beyond anything you ever imagined.

FRIENDS IN LIFE AND IN BUSINESS...

I am very blessed to call some amazing people friend and any opportunity I get the chance to spend time with them, I'm greatly appreciative. I'll be the first to say that this is not the easiest status to achieve with me. Not because I think I sit so high and mighty and look down upon other people, but it's more that friends should challenge you to be better, go farther, finish strong and when you fall help you get back up and say let's keep going. They understand what it means to win and it's not about the prize, but the process. Funny thing is I've not always been the best friend. I would always attract people, but many times I didn't pursue and take the time to build genuine relationships. Thankfully, during college, my mindset shifted and my thoughts began to change because I learned how to value myself and therefore became fully able to value other people.

The friend in business is much the same way. Respect is the quintessential lynchpin of a foundation for a friendship to take place. We in the areas and arenas of commerce must connect with respect and see the value in each other. I am a connector at heart and creative consultant by trade. I move in life as a problem solver and know exactly how to get desired results by connecting the dots that some simply just don't see. In a sense... I think it stems from childhood training where I would put puzzles together face-down thereby increasing my cognitive learning skills (Thanks, Aunt Pearl.), but nevertheless some kinda way, I put it together to make it all work. So when I have the opportunity to connect people, business and brands it creates a sense of meaning for me because now we have a bigger and even better cluster of smart and success focused individuals added to this experience we call life.

So in closing... make friends in life and be a friend in business. You'd be surprised at the impact you both make on each other and people for the rest of your lives.

THE 'SUPA DUPA' BOWL...

Today I'm 'tackling' (pun intended) The 2014 Superbowl Halftime Show. Yes, it was 'Supa Dupa Fly' with a special thanks to Missy Elliot, but what I want to address is the sideline comments of people thinking that Katy Perry was upstaged, etc.

I go back to the previous entry where we dissected Friends in Life & In Business. The main point is that when you have friends... they will look out for you when it's time. Many don't know that Missy Elliott was a part of Katy Perry's remix to Teenage Dream (Katy's fifth #1 record) back in 2011 or that she (Missy) has also helped so many artists dating back 20 years! You name it... she's worked with them from Eminem to Beyoncé to Tommy Lee to Puff Daddy and even Yolanda Adams. And these artists are not just from hip-hop, but as you can see this list includes rock, pop and gospel. As stated many times, Missy Elliott is an innovator with a heart that has served people and this past Sunday it all came to a superstar moment for her career. But had she not put in the work and made friends then... she wouldn't have been called upon to display her amazing attributes on the world's biggest stage now.

No one can take what is freely given.

I salute Katy Perry for an amazing visual display during Sunday's show. The colors and staging were very impressive. For the most part, I watched the halftime show on mute and still her visual display was spot on... especially 'left shark'. From the prismatic tiger entrance to her flying away on a shooting star, she nailed her set. I think the biggest thing that speaks to me is her character though. She's a fan of Missy and in a press conference prior to the game she said she wanted to give another artist her time to shine. This is big to me only because in a world filled with people who are dog-eat-dog and have excessive episodes of throwing people under buses... backing up over them and hitting them again... it's great to see someone be a friend in business and give one of their friends a shining moment on the world's biggest stage that literally re-invents their career. Katy Perry is Supa Dupa Fly.

5 WAYS TO INCREASE YOUR CREATIVITY...

Let's discuss Creativity and Creative Execution. It's funny, most people feel they are not creative or that they don't perform like X person and that their creative sensibilities are completely null and void. To put it simply, this is completely untrue. We all use a sense of creativity in our lives on a daily basis... I just don't think we all rationalize it to be creative. Case in point, the mom that has two kids both under the age of 5... The single guy trying to figure out how to propose... The empty nester harnessing a new lease on life... All of these situations require effective creative execution and can easily be harnessed in 5 simple ways:

1.) Listen to Music.

From Bach to Tupac and Biggie to Beethoven, music has always had a way of unlocking the imagination of vivid imagery. Personally, I listen to songs from a myriad of genres and then begin to paint a picture on the canvas of my mind based on the lyrics and emotions. This becomes highly effective when working on a client brief because I can now fully interpret their thoughts and expressions in the form of a song and allow people to see what I heard. Some time ago a friend mentioned to me, "Practice makes Permanent" and that phrase has stuck ever since. The more practice I consume the better I am when its game time.

2.) Sit in Silence.

It's Golden! This is one of those rare moments that you have to fight for, but I promise it is worth it. My favorite times are 2 a.m. if I've been up, and 4 a.m. if I'm just waking up. There is something about the fact that the world is asleep and it's just you alone with your thoughts and driven imagination.

3.) Flashback to Childhood.

One of the greatest tricks of the creative trade is to remember what you did when you were 7 and act out accordingly. Many of the coolest experiences I've created are centered around the awesome time I shared with my friends and family from youth. In a sense... people don't change. Their attitudes and likes may, but at the heart of it all, people all over the world generally want to be happy, have fun and feel loved. It's not hard to supply a universal demand.

4.) Read.

Sounds so simple, but you'd be surprised at how many people don't read books. With the advent of Facebook, Twitter and Instagram we are only using a microcosm of our mind's true potential. Read if you want to lead! There are so many stories and anecdotes that have been chronicled in the pages of a book. One of my favorite quotes and lifestyle mantra simply states, "There is nothing new under sun... Everything did has already been done."

5.) Teach.

Students will always make you more creative because they'll challenge you on the spot with a question, viewpoint or situation you never considered. I'm not just saying formalized education... This extends to mentorship and even raising kids. As a Subject Matter Expert (SME), it is your job to know it all or find it out... And if you spend enough time pouring your knowledge and information into others, more and more will always be in reserve.

Be Creative... You have it in you.

MAKE 'EM WANT MORE...

The dynamics of supply and demand... As many of you know I host high-end branded experiences and next-level marketing engagements. So recently I had the idea of hosting a series entitled Friday Night Live! which is my take on a weekend variety show similar to that of the Midnight Special, but has a different incarnation each time its presented. This past weekend was the launch and I must say it was a result of flawless execution. Technically, it was an unproven concept, but since it's not my first time at the rodeo, things turned out amazing.

For this first initiation, we created a Jazz Dinner Lounge that featured spoken word artists, vocalists and highlighted a jazz saxophonist. Think Kenny G meets Earth, Wind & Fire with a Tonight Show flare and me as the host. But here's the deal... we sold this show out without hesitation or any expectation of doing so. Now I knew it would sell out as soon as I presented the idea because I have an understanding of people and simple mathematics.

Here is the math... we only had 300 seats available with tickets starting at $35, included a four-course meal and we had a database of 20,000 people... Honestly, I wasn't worried at all, but it seems that even with all of this information being readily available... no one has ever had success in this manner with this organization. It got to the point where we had to turn people away and concluded with a waiting list of over 100 people.

End result... show was amazing and people loved it. Comments said consistently over and over again was "We'll be back!" "AMAZING!" "When is the next one?!?" "We can't wait!" To get to this point is a simple process I employ that we all can easily do on an everyday basis... Give them a Wow! factor. At the end of the day people want to be amazed and in a sense, transported back to childhood wonderment. And the simple answer is that it's not hard when you create value for them. One of my best friends has a saying that he quotes religiously... "When value exceeds price there is a sale every time." ...And I love the fact that I strive to give value to people. That is how you make 'em want more.

I say all of this to say... add value to your everyday life with every relationship that you possess. Value your business, value your time, value your friends and far beyond anything else value yourself. When you provide value and live a valued life everything around you will increase for the better.

YOU CAN'T STOP ME...

At first, I must be honest... this was going to be a depressing, 'woe is me' post. Not gonna lie... frustration had hit and I was simply tired. Tired of the fight. Tired of the faith it takes to win. Just tired of being tired. And before I even began to write some witty title of why I quit... The words just sprang forth, piercing through the encroaching elements of doubt and unbelief... "You Can't Stop Me!"

From Andy Mineo to John Cena, this is a phrase that if repeated as a mantra that you can defeat any of your greatest detractors and come out victorious. Maybe this is meant for those co-workers/employers that don't/didn't believe in you. Maybe it's meant for the family members that laughed at your dream. Or maybe it's even meant for you...

For YOU?!? Yep... for you. I don't know if you're anything like me, but I find the greatest self-motivating time is when I look in the mirror. This is the moment where I spend thought-provoking time and insight and simply share honest truth with myself. The power of the mirror is that it gives you a reflection of 'where you are'. Which is great in the moment, but we all must remember that it is our ultimate determination to decide 'where we are going'. Just because I'm not where I eventually want to be, doesn't meant I can't be thankful of where I came from.

So take time and even do a selfie if you have to and just say "You Can't Stop Me!" Here's honest truth… No one ever remembers the person that quit. Yes, it may get hard and it may be tough, but you were built for this. And everything that was done to bring destruction in your life only turned out to build you up and get prepared for the next level.

LOOK AT ME NOW...

We just talked about "The Mirror Effect" and how it is a great reflection of where you are, but not a determination of where you are going and/or are headed and many times in life... co-workers, friends and family would like to put you in a box and remind you of where you once were while forgetting the fact that you have changed, matured and developed into something and someone much different, much better and much greater... To put it simply, there has been a shift and you are not the person you used to be and its time they caught up.

This is rather effective when it comes to things of the past. Many people are stuck in the same place they were 10 years ago and never developed into something greater. We've all heard the story of the football star that peaked in high school and still has dreams of that last game that was 20 years ago... At some point you have to say I have to keep it moving. What's done is done... now it's time to have some fun.

When I use the phrase "Look At Me Now" it's not to shout and point fingers at someone else and say "Yeah... This is me. I did this!" **No!** It's me saying to myself... "Wow! I'm so thankful for everything I have because I know where I came from..."

I WANT MY MTV...

My take on MTV does not stand for Music Television rather it stands for some things that inherently relate to all of us in some form or fashion.

In this case...

MTV stands for **MONEY, TIME** and **VALUE** and begins to readily apply itself in a myriad of forms...

When dealing with or as a customer, people are concerned about these three basic points, but sadly so many people miss them.

Money- Save It & Make More Of It

Time- Don't Waste It.

Value- Create It.

So the next time you think about, "I Want My MTV!"... Remember customers, clients and friends are all screaming for the same thing from you. If you can supply it, you'll be in high demand for the rest of your life.

THE LUCK OF THE I WISH...

Raise your hand if you have found a pot of gold at the end of a rainbow yet... Don't worry it's there, but it looks a lot different than what many of us have imagined. When we talk about 'The Luck of the I Wish..." this references the fact that life is more than a simple wish. It's work, but not in the way many of us would perceive. Do we need to work hard in all we do? Absolutely, but many times we exchange the physical labor when it should really be mental labor that works the hardest.

Your mind is the fertile ground for the planting of success and many times it's easy to get distracted from your "garden"... We all must fight to keep our thoughts aligned with where we are going and not simply focused on where we are or have been. If we continuously make small improvements on a day-to-day basis we will realize that we have much more that a single pot of gold, but rather have reached the ultimate goal of lifestyle fulfillment.

Before you wish on luck... Bet on yourself.

THE RARE VIEW OF THE REARVIEW...

Focus on what's ahead because it's so easy to miss the grand opportunities before you if you are fixated on things that have already past.

IF IT MAKES YOU HAPPY...

I was recently reading an article published over at Fast Company about the value of experiences vs. physical things and I couldn't agree more. When I take a personal assessment of my life and business, it's all about people. I look forward to creating paradigm shifts in what they thought possible of things to enjoy. I celebrate life and truly believe that it is meant to be well-lived and experienced. The only true limitation on our perception of happiness is what we choose to believe.

So if it makes you happy... Do It. You will always regret those things which in the end don't mean much. Personally, my mindset is on a Ferrari California T in black, but no matter how awesome I believe this car is... it doesn't hold a candle to some of the amazing people I have in my life that I am truly able to call friend. That's a real experience... The experience of what you do will forever be enhanced by those with whom you choose to do it with.

So in closing... Be Happy.

IT'S OKAY TO BE A HERO...

What does it take to Be A Hero? I thought about it intensely and began to ask many additional questions like: Who is my hero? Whose Hero Am I? Why Am I/They A Hero? Do I Even Want to Be A Hero? So many questions that needed answers became a personal reflection of my positioning in life...

So let's take on that initial question of What Does it take to Be A Hero? My answer to this is so simple, yet complex. For me, to be a hero it just takes being yourself. Your true identity will always shine through when you are your authentic self. And to be a hero doesn't mean you need Spandex and a Six Pack, it just means that you need to care. For the longest time I didn't accept the role of a hero. I would downplay my strengths and character to blend into the background to attempt to go unnoticed, but after some time I realized that wasn't authentic to who I was and so I had to change.

I will say that being a hero is exciting and you actually do feel like Superman and it creates an element that you have something to live up to. Personally, I have friends who are my heroes. I see them being amazing fathers to their kids and awesome husbands to their wives and it means something to me. I also celebrate the heroes I find in business. I am very fortunate to be around multimillionaires on a consistent basis and what I love about most of the ones that I'm associated with is that in the process of accumulating this vast wealth, they didn't lose their families in the process. They remained a hero!

I say all of this to say… BE A HERO! If nothing else, you never know who's counting on you to succeed. Many times you are the hope for other people and a beacon of light that reflects upon them that says… YES! You can make it. Sometimes it may be hard to be a hero because you have to lead. You are the one that takes the bumps and the bruises, but I say this to you… "Don't give up because you were built for this!" Fear is your only Kryptonite.

THE POWER OF YOUR STORY...

Yes... Your Story. Many times we don't realize the breakthroughs that we have had in our own lives and how that tale of what we've been through can translate to others and serve as a means of how to get through.

Over the weekend I was afforded the opportunity to hear a few ladies share their tales of triumph amidst unimaginable tragedy. One had survived a sordid story of domestic abuse from the hands of an adopted child while another was recently divorced 2 weeks ago. In their shared pain of adversity, I watched as they bonded as sisters and pushed themselves to the next level of success in something as simple as a choreographed workout. It is amazing at how the story of one can empower others.

So I ask you... What is your story? What have you been through that can assist someone else. When we really look at it, what you went through was not completely for you, but also can serve as a cautionary tale for others. I leave you with a quote that was shared with me by my mother, "Bought Sense is the Best Kind..."

IT'S BEGINNING TO LOOK A LOT LIKE CHRISTMAS...

Contrary to popular belief, many people are not excited for the holidays. To some, it is a reminder that another year has passed and that they have not advanced or moved forward in any meaningful way towards their goals, visions or dreams and that the harsh reality is that they are still in the same place they were yesterday and the year(s) before.

At some point we all have to get excited about the life we have and recognize the gift that it is to live it. Many people aren't able to enjoy this holiday season because they are simply no longer here. Recently, I lost some friends and I'm sure I'm not alone, but now is the time to set a course to really live.

Dr. Maxwell Maltz, a plastic surgeon in the 1950s, took note that it takes a minimum of 21 days to form a new habit and went on to describe his observations in his blockbuster book, Psycho-Cybernetics. With that being said... if it takes a minimum of 21 days to form a new habit... If we start now we don't have to make a resolution January 1st that we may beat ourselves up over because we didn't fully commit to it.

Don't Put Off for Tomorrow What You Can Do Today...

RUDOLPH'S 5 LESSONS ON LEADERSHIP...

2014 marked the 75th Anniversary of the classic Christmas carol and also the 50th Anniversary of the claymation classic tale of **Rudolph, The Red-Nosed Reindeer.** (*Fun Fact: This entire song/story was created by Montgomery Ward as a marketing campaign that would later receive a #1 record thanks to Mr. Gene Autry.*)

But today it's all about the lessons we can discover from this infectious tune...

> *You know Dasher, and Dancer, and*
> *Prancer, and Vixen,*
> *Comet, and Cupid, and*
> *Donner and Blitzen*
> *But do you recall*
> *The most famous reindeer of all*

Lesson 1: It is not your job to make your name great.

Many times in life we grind it out to be "popular", but the truth is that greatness comes from servanthood. We'll get into a little more detail in a minute, but the harsh reality is that no one ever became great without serving someone else. Think about it... Moguls like Bill Gates, Steve Jobs, Sarah

Blakely, Michael Jordan, Oprah Winfrey, Andrew Carnegie all served others in the accumulation of their wealth. Side Note: Andrew Carnegie became so enthralled with serving others, his philanthropy caused a "giving war" between himself and John D. Rockefeller.

> *Rudolph, the red-nosed reindeer*
> *had a very shiny nose*
> *and if you ever saw it*
> *you would even say it glows.*

Lesson 2: There is something unique about you.

How many times have we wanted to be Bob from Accounting or Mary in HR...? In some form of human nature, many times we see the gifts/gifting that other people are equipped with and forget to focus on or try to hide our own.

> *All of the other reindeer*
> *used to laugh and call him names*
> *They never let poor Rudolph*
> *play in any reindeer games.*

Lesson 3: Leadership Can Be Lonely.

It takes a lot to lead. As a leader, you can't always hang with the crowd. The reason is because if you think just like them, you're not going to be able to take them to a place where they have never been. There are so many stories throughout time where leaders have been ostracized as outcasts only to come back into the fold and lead people beyond their imagination. 2 stories that immediately come to mind, Joseph and Moses.

> *Then one foggy Christmas Eve*
> *Santa came to say:*
> *"Rudolph with your nose so bright,*
> *won't you guide my sleigh tonight?"*

Lesson 4: Purpose will Reveal Itself.

There will come a point when it will be apparent why you work at your company. Remember, Rudolph was still a reindeer. As a correlation, there may be co-workers and office creatures that may not like you for XYZ reason, but you got hired. Trusting that you were hired by a great manager, there is a reason exactly why you are on the team. In this instance… a problem arose and there was only one person who could cut through the clutter and shine a light so bright that we could get all of these toys and gifts delivered to these kids.

> *Then all the reindeer loved him*
> *as they shouted out with glee,*
> *Rudolph the red-nosed reindeer,*
> *you'll go down in history!*

Lesson 5: Greatness Speaks for Itself.

In the end, people will tell the tale of how you saved the day. They'll be excited at the fact that YOU were on THEIR team. It's funny, it goes back to the entry entitled "The Power of Thank You"... People can't help but to tell someone else about the great deed you did because you helped them when they needed it most. And as it relates to going down in history... I imagine it means that Rudolph got a promotion. #BONUS!

WORK YOUR NET...

With it being holiday season, I imagine at this point you've probably already attended your office holiday party and hopefully you survived with your dignity and job intact. With that being said, I do hope that you have been able to take advantage of the amazing opportunities that have presented themselves in the form of networking whether inside your own organization or outside of it.

I was recently invited to attend a special presentation of Marvel Universe Live and thanks to a special connection, I enjoyed the Suite Life while watching the Spider-Man, The Incredible Hulk, Captain America, Iron Man (My favorite superhero... I think it's a first name thing.) and Thor plus more handle business in a live-action theatrical performance laying the smack down on Loki and a host of other villainous creatures and characters. Great show, but I must say it was an even better experience in the connections that I made while sharing snacks and soda from the private viewing area. These are the moments we all must take advantage of and really be super. Just because the office holiday party is over don't forget that you also have family and friends that may be able to connect you with the next opportunity where an organization needs your specific super human powers.

Remember, networking is a JOB... never be unemployed. And if no one remembers who you are, then what was their purpose in meeting you anyway?

It's About **WHAT** You Know.
It's About **WHO** You Know.
But Most Importantly...
It's About **WHO KNOWS YOU**!

THE FINAL COUNTDOWN...

What did you really accomplish this past year? I'll be the first to tell you... I don't believe in resolutions. I find that the advent of making a "change" on a predestined date only to revert back to a previous lifestyle is essentially a waste of time. Rather than to be inundated with millions of other mid-January revelers with abandonment, I've decided to look at this upcoming year in a completely different perspective.

For the past 3, going on 4 years I have been a "Big" with Big Brothers, Big Sisters and this past week issued a challenge to my "Little" that somewhat defied the traditional resolution approach. I simply said to him... list 3 goals to accomplish for 2015 and we will do whatever it takes to accomplish them. No resolution, but an end point and destination. The setup is to hit a goal and then set and make another one. By the end of the year we have a real-time progress tracker of where we are headed and what it takes to not only get there, but stay there and be great!

Honestly, I am expecting one of the greatest years of my life over the next 12 months! It's not that everything is perfect as it is, but I've set my mind that its already done. I feel like Ice Cube back in '93 kicking the lyrics to "It Was a Good Day"... Shake

'Em Up, Shake 'Em Up, Shake 'Em Up, Shake 'Em. I am in great expectation for not only my life but that of my family and friends. I guess it feels good to be a gangsta.

.

WHAT'S IN A NAME...

This past weekend I was in Augusta, Georgia for the inauguration festivities surrounding the city's newest mayor and I must say it was time well spent. This meet and greet was very important to me because as it stands today, for one week during the month of April, Augusta, Georgia has the eyes of the entire world cast upon it for it is home to the most prestigious event in modern sports history... The Masters' Golf Tournament.

In preparation for our visit, I had the opportunity to speak with the mayor as we planned details for the trip. Being introduced via a third party, his first question to me was "Did I know XYZ Rouse?" I chuckled and replied, "Yes. That is my mother." He then proceeds to mention to our shared connection, "if this is the person you're dealing with, then they are cut from some very good cloth!"

As we continued the conversation I couldn't help but think about the power of a name. What sat with me most was that I had favor(s) simply because of association. The way my mother treated people carried over to my life and gave me access into places where I previously knew of no entry point as well and then it made me question character as it related to how I treated people. The biggest takeaway I had was that Character is not something we are born with, but rather it is built. Over and over again via our everyday interactions with those around us. It is the one thing that we can change to be better and keep it for the rest of our lives.

Maybe at this moment in time your character is not the greatest or your reputation is not one of integrity. Know that you have the power to create and change, but most importantly... reflect the characteristics you want to display. It's your life. Live it and if nothing else... be it. Money can do many things, but a great name with access and association(s) can do even more.

BEST OF THE BEST...

What would happen if you decided to be the best in the world at what you do?!?

To be honest, this is something that I never fully considered. Don't get me wrong, I've always strived to be the best in what I did... whether it was winning industry awards or garnering national recognition, but this question posed and phrased as it is, has given me an entirely different perspective on "What does it mean to be the best in the world?" Not saying that we must seek out competition with other people, but if we really pushed ourselves to unimaginable levels of greatness what is really possible?!? I think about people like hotel and resort magnate Steve Wynn, otherworldly entrepreneur Richard Branson, sports icon Michael Jordan (when he played basketball, not baseball... we forget '94 and '95 on purpose) and say wow these people were/are literally the best at what they do. Then I begin to think if they can exceed in their fields, why can't I.

I say to you be the best of the best. Realize it's not where you come from that defines you, but rather your decision to be great will be the ultimate reflection of a life well-lived. Don't let your potential be permanent.

IF I NEVER SAID IT...

As I join you today I've been very reflective over a few things, but one in particular that sits with me very strong is the presence of people. I say this to reference the old adage that actions speak louder than words... And use it as a juxtaposition to announce, "What are you really saying?!?"

If we are who we all say we are... then it should intrinsically line up with everything that we do. A quote from a good friend of mine simply states that "Rich People Yell... Wealthy People Whisper." I find this very interesting because when its wealth, you don't have to make a grandiose scene to let people know. It easily can be observed by the movements.

I also choose to have this define my personal life at the moment that if I know who I am, my actions will inherently speak for themselves when I go to deal and interact with other people... Who I am is truly defined by what I do.

So I say to all of you... tell those that are watching you... "Pay Attention." And to reference Trinidad James and Bruno Mars... "Don't Believe Me Just Watch." If I Never Said It... Would You Even Know??? If my actions speak louder than words, then the simple response should be... "No Explanation Necessary."

THE COMPLEXITY OF NO...

"No."

We've all heard it at some point. Maybe it was when closing a sale or if we flashback to high school when you finally got up the courage to ask someone out... but let's be honest, you've heard the word "No."

I love the references in the great sales books that say "No is the first step to yes!" But I tend to look at it a little differently. When presenting an opportunity where you could get a response of a "No." or "Yes." Have you ever thought about how you can make your customers say "Yes." from the beginning?!? I can't even begin to describe the amount of ill-prepared presenters and presentations that I have had to deal with when it comes to conversations surrounding sponsorship and other topics of monetary means.

Here's the thing... Tell then Sell. Meaning that if you are trying to pitch something, tell a story. If I'm not engaged, then I'm not buying. Also remember that this is not about you!!! Yes... in the end its about you getting what you want, but if you focus on that and not on the buyer then you both lose because you have no sale and no result. Don't forget... No is a complete sentence and if you hear it don't spaz out. It simply means you didn't come correct in this moment. Step Back. Gather yourself and approach again. Who knows… your buyer may be more receptive when you have your act together…

HUMILITY IS EVERYTHING...

Today is such a great day to be alive and reflect on the amazing journey and adventure we call life. I join you with a simple understanding that humility is everything... Nothing much more to be added to this.

REMEMBER TO REST...

Recently I have been going non-stop with project after project and not taking the time for a significant break in between. I would wake up get ready for work and at many stretches go for multiple episodes of seven days in a row on end because I would always be involved with something. Funny thing is that all of that changed this past weekend with a nap in the park. For the first time in many months I didn't have any pressing appointment, assignment or deliverable for a three-hour period and I loved every minute of it.

What I and many of my compatriots do is work... ALOT. Sometimes it's in the form of service with no payment or its striving to hit that quota multiplier that creates the additional bonus payouts for the month, but it's all work. What I learned even as simple as a moment in the park is that I have to rest. Resting is a very interesting concept in that it's really means to 'STOP'. To 'STOP' also meant that you had to be going at some point... Let me be clear: It's okay to rest after you've worked, but if you haven't worked you have no reason to rest.

But here's the thing... we have to rest. At some point our bodies need rejuvenation and the days of no-sleep til Sunday get old really quick! I say this to you as I'm also training myself... take the time to rest. Your body will thank you for it and your family will as well. It's amazing what quality time can do for any strained situation. And my last point is this… when you rest that is saying that you trust.

Many ancient civilizations use the analogies of vegetation to explain situations and scenarios because they were a part of an agrarian society… So the best way to explain rest is like that of a seed. A seed is at rest after its planted, but once planted can produce far beyond anything ever imagined. Think about it… a watermelon seed contains an entire lineage of watermelons, but can never achieve its full potential unless it is put to 'rest'.

In closing… Live your life, but remember to rest. When at rest… things really do start to happen and in the case of a watermelon seed can multiply and magnify far beyond your imagination. Now apply that same thought process to your life and actions and I personally believe you now really have something to talk about.

SPRINT TO THE FINISH...

I remember the Nintendo Power Pad like it was yesterday... my cousins and I would do our best to take on the best athletes around the Nintendo World in a foot (and hand) race to the finish. From Turtle to Bear to Horse and the ultimate challenge Cheetah! (Now mind you we did use our hands a little bit because Cheetah was really a challenge... Always Utilize Your Resources...)

Which brings us to our topic of today... Sprint to the Finish. Recently I was faced with some major challenges and things at the time would seem insurmountable. In truth... I wanted to quit, but had to face facts that I couldn't. Not that I would have to make some grand announcement about it, but deep down I'd know that had I given up when it got tough, I couldn't honestly continue to write these posts or deliver insight and encouragement with authenticity. Could I have failed... yes, but the ultimate failure is when you quit! So when I realized the only way was through, I laced up the kicks and dug deep and pressed on in.

What was so amazing is that when I decided that there was no turning back I began to pick up steam. I saw the finish line and then it was on like Donkey Kong! I knew that if nothing else people would know "I was here." I say all of this to say that... Yes, trials and challenges are going to come. It is going to look bleak, but press. Dig deep and sprint to the finish. Life is a marathon, but at each juncture there is a finish line. Know that you are about to go from one race to the next, but you finished the last one in first place and you can and will do it again.

BAND OF BROTHERS...

Jesus had his 12. Leonidas had his 300. Kanye, Big Sean and Jay-Z rapped about it in Clique and it's one of the coolest things you can experience in life. Today the topic is Brotherhood. For those that understand this phenomena of Bro Life, I welcome you into the inner sanctuary and to others here is a front-row seat...

It's funny... I hype this up to sound so complex, but in all actuality its very simple... Brotherhood comes down to respect and alignment of purpose. As a dude, it's easy for me to walk with you whether we be in a war fighting alongside each other or in the process of moving your furniture. The connecting bond is a defined goal and/or plan. Not a hard process to understand, but it must be defined. Confusion works for no one and if I'm going to spend my Saturday afternoon helping someone else... it better be planned out so I know and understand the investment of my time.

The one thing about true Brotherhood is that you celebrate the success of other people. When they win, we all win. It becomes a moment of selflessness and not selfishness. At this time, many of my connects are experiencing moments of transition. Some are about to start new roles within their current companies and others have started their own companies. I have some that have recently purchased lake houses and others that are moving into their first house. All that being said, I am thankful for the connections and bonds of success that extend beyond friendship. If nothing else, it makes a great story of achievement because as a collective... iron sharpens iron.

THINGS MY FATHER SAID...

"Get Up." "Fight." "Don't Quit." "Think." "Slow Down." "Speed Up." "Pause." "Stop." "No. Really Stop." "Why?" "Because I said so." "If that's how you feel..."

I've thought about this post for quite some time and it all came back to the lessons I learned early on in life. I'm thankful to say that I appreciate my dad. I think we all had our time figuring out this thing called life, but as evidenced by the many phrases above... we didn't quit, but believe me I wanted to... many, many times. I think as with most of us, it all comes down to perseverance and the reality of identity, but for me this also goes back to my grandfather and his father and even to even his father...

As a child, I learned that I am a direct descendant of slaves on my father's side (And like every other African-American that claims it... Native American as well. Jokes!). My great great grandfather was born into a life of servitude, but did see freedom with his own children and now generations to come. Of course I didn't understand it all as much then as I do now, but even in that premise I find thankfulness in the fact that because they endured… my entire family now lives free.

I don't know the exact conversations that my great great grandfather had and it's possible that I will never know, but what I do know is that the spirit and will to succeed has been something that is ingrained in my identity. From my grandfathers' approach to singing on Sunday mornings to my father's approach of helping me understand what he does with nuclear engineering, I am thankful to be a man in a line of men that endured so that others could gain. So as best I can describe it... the old adage rings true actions speak louder than words and many times what you don't say, actually says more than what you do...

TEAMWORK MAKES THE D.R.E.A.M. WORK...

Recently, I was honored with the opportunity to deliver a presentation at the annual Summer Leadership Summit for a select group of rising high school juniors and seniors. The topic of conversation was how to be a leader and what could they do to improve or establish their own next-level leadership skills. As you all will soon see, this became a session that we all would learn from. Let me explain...

Leadership is that one thing that we all have potential for and essentially should demonstrate in some form everyday throughout our lives. It is the one constant that dictates the level of success or failure that we will or can achieve because it simply serves as the feedback as to how we can all handle, approach and respond to any given situation. My take during this discussion was to address the benefits of leading a team and the manner of how it all can work in tandem with one another.

Have you ever been a part of a group that had a major tendency to get stuck before it ever even started? Before we establish any momentum and movement of a team, we have to define what the task is. Confusion is one of my biggest pet peeves. I can't stand the fact of disorganization when it comes to execution. Reason why is because as I mentioned before on this forum... I value my time. The dream in and of itself is a vision, goal or plan that is set to mark an intended destination, but without having an established territory plotted and/or planned out we have no frame of reference for what we are really after.

From the point of defining what we are after, we then move to the arena of designing what it should look like. Many times we often know where we are going, but many times the complicated issues that come up is "how" to get there... Teamwork makes the D.R.E.A.M. work because we are all in this together and without you "we" are nothing.

A NEW BEGINNING...

Take an assessment of where you are and compare it to where you thought or wanted to be. If you can see that the path is not shaping up like you expected, you may want to check your inputs. The definition of insanity is doing the same things over again and expecting a different result. If you were a farmer of apple trees you wouldn't plant the seeds of oranges. I say all of this to say... It is your choice whether you finish strong. Be better than you were before and relentlessly pursue the vision that you have for yourself and your life.

A MOMENT IN TIME...

Lately I've been very reflective as it relates to opportunities that we all have set before us. I can't help but to pinpoint those times when it seems that a turning point is near. Yes, I have great friends and family who all get excited about some of the cool things I'm able to do, but I feel there is a major shift underway we all should be anticipating. Personally, it is similar to the post of last week were we discussed New Beginnings and I think that they are now more apparent and prevalent than ever before.

Imagine right now at this very time and very place, what decision could you make that would radically change your life for the better?

It's actually not that hard to do and in a way that was a trick question. You are in control of your life... So whatever decision you make is just that. Not saying that there aren't other factors that affect you, but more so what do you have an effect on? And that it is you and your choice to choose.

I recently had a session where someone told me they made a bad decision. We acknowledged it and came to the reality that it was in the past and that we were going to make great decisions moving forward. So many times people beat themselves up for years over silly things that have no real effect on their future. The difference between a great warrior and a loser is that when a warrior gets knocked down 7 times... he stands up 8.

WHEN DISASTER STRIKES...

Outside of it being one of my favorite Busta Rhymes albums (Songs featured include: Put Your Hands Where My Eyes Can See & Dangerous)... "When Disaster Strikes" means that at some point, you may be faced with one of the toughest challenges you have yet to see on your journey. It could come in the form of job loss, personal/family/business problems or all of the above in any grand magnitude. One question I always ask myself when a major situation or setback comes up is: "What Are You Going To Do?" And with that I am always reminded of the quote from Charles Swindoll, "Life is 10% what happens to you and 90% of how you react to it."

This past weekend I was completing a project for a client and disaster struck in a major way. The task was to find and broker a deal for an event space so that they could host a showcase for some of their industry partners and friends. Doesn't sound too hard until you take in consideration I had less than 24 hours to complete this task and it was right before the 4th of July weekend and the show was in 10 days... Now I could have found the location and stopped there, but I believe that bare minimum will leave you with the bare minimum and so I stayed on the project just to ensure a proper handoff because this was new territory for all parties involved... And sure enough for some strange reason at the last minute the air conditioning system in the building completely crashed the day of the show without enough time to have a professional correct the problem.

Let me preface a few things... Atlanta, Ga is warm in the winter and in this case, we are talking JULY... Couple that with a few hundred people in an enclosed area and things can get uncomfortable very quickly. But again we go back to the "What Are You Going To Do?" Thankfully, we had a great team and a last-minute game plan...

First, we <u>addressed the situation</u> head on. As a point of insight: Anytime you are dealing with a crisis or problem don't shy away from action, but assess, address and then act. Assessment is necessary because it causes a time to think before you proceed. Once we realized there was no time to have the system fixed we proceeded to inform the attendees of the situation to better prepare them for what was to come.

Second, we <u>acted on what we could</u>. As a team we knew that the guests were going to be very warm while inside the area so instead of throwing our hands up with a Kanye Shrug we began serving ice-cold water to help ease the current situation. When you run into a brick wall... either break it down or find a way around.

And last, we <u>apologized for the inconvenience</u>. One of my favorite sayings is that, "People Don't Care How Much You Know Until They Know How Much You Care." What we all realize is that yes unfortunate events may take place that no one plans for (system was fine prior to day of show), but the response is what will always make or break a business or brand.

I am happy to say that while this situation was not ideal in the best sense at all, we were able to at least mitigate risk in the form of action-oriented resolve and move forward with integrity intact.

LET'S GIVE THEM SOMETHING TO TALK ABOUT...

A few months ago I was asked to be a part of a national conference scheduled to take place in Atlanta, Ga. The excitement that I have comes from the fact that this conference is built for the entire family, but the core audience is teenagers. I'm sure that at the very mention of the word 'teenager' many of us have flashbacks to episodes 10, 20, 30, 40 and even 50 years ago where we remember where we were and what it felt like to be in high school and go through all of the scenarios from games to graduation and all of the cast of characters we met along the way... but the funny thing is... we all remember what it was like: The coming into your own, the understanding of perception versus reality and the establishment of identity. As I now work with teenagers on a consistent basis in addition to my other areas of involvement... let me be the first to tell you that things haven't changed one bit. I will say technology and the internet has accelerated the process as it relates to the access of information, but the same insecurities and familiar know-it-all mindset still exists. Besides, I believe we don't fully 'grow-up' until 26 anyway...

Whatever it is that you go to do in life you should always strive to be memorable. That's not to say that you are desperate for attention (Many are aware of my disdain for people at networking events that are 'too thirsty'.), but rather that you make a great first impression that will have people remember exactly who you are. As a personal reference... there is a reason my website, Instagram, Twitter, etc. is branded with 'Meet Tony Rouse'. I want visitors to know that when they connect with me it will always be for a memorable and enjoyable experience. It is always about the experience. Never forget that.

Whether I'm in my role as a Sr. Product Manager designing user-centered interactives, a Branding Specialist for Fortune 500 companies or a Creative Consultant working on the world's next-level engagement... it is ALWAYS about the experience. It reminds me of the saying by the amazing late Dr. Maya Angelou that I apply to everything that I do... "I've learned that people will forget what you said, people will forget what you did, but people will never forget how you made them feel."

WHAT ARE YOU MADE OF?!?

To be very transparent, this would have seemed to be one of the most challenging times I've personally faced because there is a lot of transition currently going on, but to the contrary... it has only built me up because I know what's inside of me and to put it simply: "I was built for this..." My optimism is at an all-time high and to be honest it's kind of intoxicating. I never been one to seek out a fight, but when I realized I was in one to better myself, I had the simple resolve of "Game On." I say all of this to say, "When the pressure is on... Do you know what you are made of???" Pressure will burst pipes, but it also makes diamonds. When you are called to step up on your job, organization or whatever and hit a "home run", will you be ready? Here's my advice: Stay ready so you don't have to get ready and know that your time is coming... Before you even realize it... it's probably already here.

SO YOU HAD A MELT DOWN...
NOW WHAT?!?

It's funny... I think in this day and age we tend to forget that moments of heightened pressure can happen, and before we even realize it, we've reached a tipping point and find ourselves scrambling for recovery from a situation that seemingly was under control. The thing is... you will have moments whether working on a product, project or in life in general where you need to let off some steam and in the process could even have a major break down. The point of discovery is not the break down, although this defines the breaking point, but rather the recovery time. And here's the thing... Just because you have a break down... it doesn't mean you're broken. So I wanted to take this time to highlight 3 things you can do to create a renewed start and dramatically decrease your recovery time:

1. **Accept** the fact that you had a moment.

Whether you chose to cry out of anger, scream out of frustration or exert extreme physicality out of aggression... know that you went "there" and that's okay.

2. **Ask** for forgiveness.

Most people would see this and say it wasn't my fault... so-and-so pushed me. Barring the fact that you inflicted physical damage on another object, I'm saying to ask forgiveness of yourself and realize this was a place you didn't necessarily intend to get to, but since we're here just say, "Self... I'm Sorry."

3. **Acknowledge** that it's time to move forward.

Recovery time is important. Personally after a major moment I just need a nap. I'm like a 3rd grader with a tantrum sometimes and it's as you would imagine... he needs a nap. Even after I've played hard on the field with high levels of exertion, I need that recovery time. To others it may be a process of three days or a week. But the thing is you have to get back up and finish what you started.

And besides... from a branding perspective remember there was a Formula 408 before what we now know of as Formula 409.

In other words... Keep Going.

STAND STILL...

As a driven individual, I am always one of those people that want to make something happen. I feel it is my task and responsibility to always be a 'playmaker', to come through in the clutch, etc. And while this is true in my style and approach to life... I have recently been reminded that in many situations I've done all I can do and I have to trust that the rest is just going to happen.

Case in point... I'm an avid fan of football. If I were a wide receiver (like Julio Jones of the Atlanta Falcons that beat the Philadelphia Eagles last night for the season opener of Monday Night Football that was broadcast to millions...) the only thing I'm responsible for is making sure I'm open and catch the ball when the quarterback throws it to me. I am responsible for three things: run my route, beat my defender and catch the ball. Outside of that, I can't control anything else. I have to trust that the offensive live blocked the defensive advancements, that my quarterback can see me on the field to place the ball appropriately and hope that this entire process works when everyone handles their assignments.

Are you that person that stresses out because there are so many factors outside of your control?!? This is the moment you just need to 'stand still'. Trust and know that you've done all that you can do and the rest is not up to you. The only thing you are responsible for is to 'be ready' so you don't have to 'get ready'. Trust that your quarterback sees you and will get you the ball... you just need to be in the right place, at the right time and most importantly... ready to go.

DRIVEN...

When I think about great advertising slogans, catchphrases and taglines that move me to action, I can't help but to look to the automobile industry for inspiration. Maybe it is something about these beautiful machines taking hairpin turns at 100 mph or the fact that in certain cars 130 feels like 55 on a back country road. Whatever the case, this industry has nailed it when it comes down to "Moving You Forward" (That was Toyota right there.). Here are a few of my favorites:

"Never Follow." - Audi
"Unlike Any Other." - Mercedes-Benz
"The Relentless Pursuit of Perfection." - Lexus
"Porsche, There is No Substitute." - Porsche

What I find in these slogans is not mere words, but an ideal that says that this product we have created doesn't just transport you from one location to the next, but rather it is an entire experience that you are able to engage with along the way. And this is the case in our very lives from a position as business and personal brand agents... What drives us? And what is that thing that drives others towards us? Is it because we are people that "Never Follow."? Or could it be the fact that there simply is "No Substitute." for who we are and what we innately do.

NO STRINGS ATTACHED...

We are not talking 'NSYNC's record-breaking sophomore album, but rather from an aspect of both business and personal observation... when was the last time you set someone up for success without any obligation of a return from them? The worst feeling in the world is for someone to feel like they are being controlled by a 'Puppet Master' with specific ramifications if they do not oblige to the strong suggestions coming from the one pulling the so-called 'strings'.

"Give the advantage. Don't be so quick to take it."
-Tony Rouse

"BYE BYE BYE"
(That was too easy...)

A RACIAL REALITY...

Before I even get too deep into this conversation... the one thing that I'd like to address is that this may be one of the most complex things I've yet to discuss on this forum. The reason being is because Takeover Tuesday is used as an educational empowerment platform with comedic elements that relate to "Business, Brands and You..." with that being said... The entire situation of race is very relevant in the workplace because that's where many groups of people come together on a consistent basis and the story that I'm about to dissect comes from... The Workplace.

So here's the story... A millennial office worker snaps a selfie of himself and a co-workers' 3-year-old child. Posts it as a profile pic on Facebook and then he and his friends then begin a racially charged exchange with comments such as they didn't know he has become a slave owner, referred to the child as Toby and Kunta Kente and then he even goes on to call the child feral. Result is he gets fired and now the fallout happens with apologies and expressions of unintended circumstances.

Here's the deal... people have a hard time accepting the fact that they are responsible for their behavior. Some may say this was on a private computer, but when you participate in the exploitation, endangerment and racial degradation of a 3-year-old on a social network that reaches billions of people what do you really expect?!? We can play this "Sorry... I didn't know..." card all day long, but let's be real about the situation... It'd be one thing if your friends went on this racially-charged route and you shut it down, but then to have you join in leaves too many questions of character and intention.

As an individual, I can't make people hate me or love me because of my skin color. It is my hope that they see who I am and what I do first, but often times we don't want to think that deep and to be honest, I'm not that naive and wandering off in La-La Land to not understand the harsh reality of the world we live in and the places we work. It's funny how all of this even relates to things such as current events. Case in point, McGraw-Hill just released a new text book that says that Europeans brought 'workers' over from Africa... No. They were workers alright, but it wasn't like people were put on a cruise ship and just happened to land in America on a permanent vacation...

The problem that we have yet to face is that we continue to put a Band-Aid and gauze strips on a malignant tumor that should have been fully exorcised 150 years ago. People can't heal from something that doesn't get treated and/or exposed. So as a step forward, realize that people aren't bloodhounds looking to point the finger at sincere racial ignorance, but rather they are very tired of veiled cloaks of lies and malicious behavior that get washed away with an "Oops... My bad."

FIGHT...

The title alone says it all... "Fight!". Not that we all have to go and get shredded like Brad Pitt's character of Tyler Durden in "Fight Club", but in a sense when it all comes down to being beat up and sometimes being beat down by everything we all face in life... just remember your will to win... and fight. Too often we quit before we see breakthrough and many times we only have to push just a little bit harder and we'll cross the finish line as a true champion. In business and in life remember... 'be a victor, not a victim.'

WHEN ONE DOOR CLOSES...

Rejection... Who is really a fan of it?!? Not only does it sting in the moment, but for some strange reason it makes you evaluate your entire existence in life. From a job perspective you may have heard, "Oh, You're Overqualified..." or "Sorry, You're Underqualified..." and then in some instances you hear nothing at all and then are relegated to the black pit of nothingness and blank space that we refer to as the internet or specifically... Taleo. But cheer up, so many times what we think is perfect may indeed be perfect for someone else. I can't tell you the amount of projects and jobs I've submitted for that I have gotten the feedback of what I didn't want to hear, especially when I thought "This is perfect for me!" In reality the only true perfect thing for any of us is when we take our unique gifting and abilities and amplify them in the workplace and in everyday life.

I love the stories of great people who took their uniqueness and amplified them like Marci Shimoff who is the author of "Happy For No Reason". Marci was always "happy" and she turned that into a very profitable business of sharing her joy with the world. She became a New York Times best-selling author from something she innately did. You too can be beacon of hope for people in whatever industry and engagement.

I'll be honest... it took me some time to realize this, but it's similar to our discussion on 'The Complexity of No'. What you think may be perfect for you at the time, may in reality be an ill-fitted format for your brand of operation. When one door closes, find the next one and kick it open or use just your key. Knocking is great when you want to be polite, but it doesn't make sense to knock on a door to a house that already belongs to you.

A SCARY THOUGHT...

Richard Branson, CEO of The Virgin Group and a Big Brother in Business, had a post from his team that profiled the prolific US businessman, John D. Rockefeller and his life prior to his wealth accumulation. As previously mentioned, Rockefeller and Andrew Carnegie famously engaged in a "give-off" throughout their lives as major philanthropists, but the one thing that this article highlighted and stood out to me was his propensity to tithe. I found this very interesting because all throughout history we see those that share indeed have more to share, but what we should really take note of, is that his charitable habit didn't BEGIN when he had BILLIONS (in today's dollars), but rather when he only had nickels and dimes. The article also goes on to highlight his charitable nature with the giving of gifts of dimes to children.

The other historical figure, I'd like to highlight is my very own grandfather. This past Sunday, I had the pleasure and opportunity to visit my grandfathers' church and hosted their 'Family & Friends Day'. The highlight of this session for me was that during the final remarks as my grandfather addressed the entire congregation, he was speaking directly to me and imparting wisdom that seemed so simple, but was truly life changing in that very moment. He simply went on to say, 'Tony... you have so many options in life, but do what brings joy to you and others as you serve God.' What I thought was most amazing in this moment was his highlight to the reference of joy as it relates to other people...

What I noticed courtesy of John D. Rockefeller and My Grandfather as I made my way back home was that when you give to others from that which you have, your life is just that much better because of it. We all have something we can give or share. It could be monetary or even just that of time, but give something. Don't wait until the moment that you are billionaire or well-seasoned in your years to finally give back... start now and watch it grow. And in that... that is when I realized the scary thought: '...That we would have waited our entire lives to make an impact on this world without just starting where we are now with what we have.'

FAITH IN BUSINESS...

Sometimes it looks impossible... honestly it probably is... to and for everyone else... but for you it is possible!

IMPOSSIBLE = I'M POSSIBLE.

AT YOUR SERVICE...

What does it mean to roll out the red carpet? What does it mean to make people feel special? What does it mean when someone goes the extra mile to attend to your very specific details? I think we all would say that it just feels great! It means something when people recognize us and our needs and makes a very concerted effort to attend to them... And this my friends is service. The most interesting thing about service is that the person that is serving chooses to make your needs more important than their own at that time. And here's the kicker... this is what leads to great success for businesses and brands. It is not a position of less than and/or have to, but rather a position of I get to or as the phrase I prefer, 'Allow Me.'

So I ask you, "When was the last time you served others, other than yourself?" And this is not just some plea for community service sign-ups or anything, but think of it in this manner: have you served at your job? Does your employer or in this case 'client' see you as a person of service that adds amazing value to their organization that propels and pushes them forward or are you simply present? Serve. It is the only way to truly become great. You see it throughout the lives of Mega-Moguls of today and those days that have gone by. Oprah Winfrey, Steve Jobs, T.D. Jakes, Tony

Robbins, Mother Teresa and more have all served people whether it was directed at their technological needs, need for humanity or just a need for connection. So as you continue the rest of your day... simply remember to 'Serve'.

THE ASSASSINATION OF MEDIOCRITY...

Point 1: Average is simply defined is being the Best of the Worst and the Worst of the Best. The question is how long do you want to dwell in the land of average? We were created to win and win consistently. Is it easy? Actually yes, but not initially. That is why people quit. We are all a part of the microwave generation and expect things at the push of a button. Look at Twitter... its instant information, but when you're plotting out success you have to plan for tomorrow while correcting course today. Do yourself a favor... plan for tomorrow, but begin fixing the issue today. It is always better to be known as the Best of the Best as opposed to the Best of the Worst.

Point 2: It comes as a revelation to me how so many individuals don't forecast their future. Are you headed where you said you were going? If not, change directions or in extreme cases, completely change your course. You have 3 options...

Complain: You're not happy were you are so you voice it to other people. Pro: You make yourself feel better in the interim Con: You are only deceiving yourself because the truth is no one cares about complainers and do not want to be around them.

Maintain: You have achieved satisfaction. Pro: Achievement is met. Con: Complacency can kill you...

Change Your Plane: On to the Next One... Pro: You take your life to another level. Con: If it was easy everyone would do it. You must refocus your objectives daily. Continue toward your dream in the face of adversity and you will achieve your destination.

Point 3: And for those that want a great reference... I Peter 2:9.

But ye are a chosen generation, a royal priesthood, a holy nation, a peculiar people; that ye should shew forth the praises of him who hath called you out of darkness into his marvelous light.

Point 4: I think the greatest thing that we all must remember is that a standard has been set.

We were called kings since the very beginning and with this being the case, why should we resort to living the life of a pauper or a pauper-ish mentality.

I think when you think of a king, of course immediately you can go to treasures, etc. But I'm also focused on justice and the wisdom of proper leadership.

I imagine my house as a throne and my life is a kingdom and if nothing else the greatest part about that kingdom is the presence of peace.

THE 4 POWER PLAYS OF SUCCESS...

Over the weekend I had the opportunity to read the newest edition of Men's Health magazine and in the October issue, Superbowl superstar Russell Wilson (QB for the Seattle Seahawks) is the front man on the cover. Already being a fan of his, I was eager to dive into the article and was ready to share some of the insight contained within.

One of the coolest things about this article is that it talked about his shortcomings as it relates to a traditional NFL QB. The main highlight was that he was too short. Stacking in at 5'11, it was said he would have a hard time seeing over the O-line and this would cause issue with taking snaps and scoring. The best part of this though was the juxtaposition contained in the article about David and Goliath. With Russell being compared to David... What was later discovered was that he actually had oversized hands making him well versed in the pigskin. They related the article to the aspect of having things hidden in plain sight and went on to further explain that when you are equipped it doesn't matter what the "average" thing is to do. The one thing it made me think about was the verse in I Samuel 16:7 where it says man looks on the outside, but God looks at the heart.

Later Wilson goes on to talk about his thoughts on success and that is where I really tuned in…

1. Visualize Success.

As men, we often seem like we're genetically wired to wing it. Sure, we study for tests, hit a bucket of balls at the range before the company golf tournament, and review our PowerPoint slides before the make-or-break presentation. But there's another step we could take to increase our chances of success.

"I'm a big visualization person," Wilson says. His hours on the practice field, in the gym, and in the video room aren't enough for him. He also spends time imagining how that preparation will play out on game day. "I'm big on note cards, and I'll sometimes go out on the field late at night. I'll call the plays in my head and walk 'em out. It's what I need to do to be successful."

2. Don't Visualize Failure.

You can't be fully prepared for success without a sense of all the ways your project can get sacked. To Wilson, there's a fine line between visualizing failure--something he says he never does--and imagining worst-case scenarios at key moments. "They get me prepared for plan B," he says. "But I never visualize failing when something goes wrong. I visualize how can I be successful."

3.Be Clear But Not Too Specific About Your Goals.

After the NFL Combine in 2012, Wilson knew that his critics were focused on his height, something he couldn't control. So on the return flight from the Combine, he wrote up a list of his goals, both for the coming season and for the future beyond, including how he wants people to remember him. He brought that list with him to Seattle and kept it in his locker.

He won't say what the list includes, only what it doesn't. "They're never statistical goals," he explains, "They're motivational goals. How I practice. How I prepare. Things I can control versus things others control."

4. Tune Out The Noise.

It's one thing to know what people are saying about you in general. But it's another to take in that criticism in granular detail or to give it undue weight in your career path. "I don't pay attention to that stuff," Wilson says. "I don't read any articles, good or bad. So I won't even read yours. I'll tell you right now."

For Wilson, ignoring the noise that comes with a high-profile career is an expression of self-confidence rather than a sign of hubris. "I know who I am," he explains. "I know my talent level. I know what I can and can't do. I try to work on my game every day, and I don't let distractions get to me."

CHECK YOURSELF...

Image is Everything. Not just in terms of superficial status, but in terms of how you view yourself and life. What happens on the inside is foretold on the outside? Wanna revamp your life? Change what you are putting into it.

3 Areas that Control Change:

The Eyes: *What are you looking at that has reshaped your thinking?* **The Ears:** *What are you listening to that has revamped your mind?* **The Mouth:** *What are you saying that is bringing about the current results that you are experiencing?*

It's just like working out... the only six pack you can get in a day will probably come from Wal-Mart. When you start to control these "gatekeepers" and regulate the flow of information, you transform your destiny. Just because you started going one way, doesn't mean you cannot change direction or even courses for that matter.

So check yourself and revamp that visual stimulation as to control auditory sensation so that you can bridle verbal communication and then receive mental, physical and spiritual gratification.

GAME TIME...

Many people are still waiting for the perfect conditions to fulfill their purpose and passion in life. Today, I challenge you to take a step in the direction of where you see yourself or where you want to be. If not now, when? Make a decision that it is Game Time!

Reference: He who watches the wind will not sow and he who watches the clouds will not reap.

- Ecclesiastes 11:4

THERMOSTAT OR THERMOMETER...

Temperature check 1-2, 1-2. So without reading any further... what would say you and your life represent? A Thermostat or a Thermometer?

The difference? A thermostat sets the temperature and makes the environment that surrounds it adjust. A thermometer is a reflection of the current standings. It adjusts to its surroundings and is a direct reflection of them. So the bigger question on the table is that in your life do you plan to be affected or effective? Affected means that you allow external forces rule your internal life. Effective means that internal forces set the standard for external environments and won't relent until the internal standards are met externally.

In closing... set your sights and maintain course until your surroundings are a reflection of your ultimate destination.

REPLAY YOUR VICTORY...

And this is how the story goes... Back in 2010 I launched my first major high-end experience called The Atlanta Food Rave. This event cost about $50,000 *(Yeah...Thank God for sponsors and wireless internet!)* to produce and honestly, I had no clue what I was in for. I was underfunded, over budget, inexperienced, hardheaded, brash and bold. The only thing I knew was that in some way shape or form, this thing that was in my head for 2 years had to come to life and I was determined to make it happen. A part of it was that I was tired of living my life at the status quo. I dreamed so much bigger and I set out to make that dream a reality. I wanted and needed an exit strategy from the life that I didn't love. I was focused and determined to pull this thing off at any all cost and it nearly cost me everything I had.

Needless to say, I took my time in the development. I calculated the movement of this experience from the very first touch point to the very last. From website interaction to menus to live entertainment, I took my time to bring my dream to life. Thank God for having help along the way in the form of friends and my dad as investors *(Paid back with 25% interest... I was generous.)* In the end, had an awesome party and the results: I won The Best

Social Event of 2011 from The International Special Events Society and was also nominated for Atlanta Marketer of the Year for Best in Event Marketing. Because of the amazing PR team I had in place, we garnered over 130 Million Media impressions and received buzz and mentions internationally in Germany and South America about people being interested in what we were doing here, how I created The Food Rave, etc. I was new to the scene and I had arrived or so I thought... I will say that I studied my craft. The Food Rave was just an extension of everything I had learned from hosting shows and entertaining people. I knew what to do without knowing what to do. In some strange way I understood luxury and premium products and knew how to create them without thinking too much about it. Then came the repeat...

So with the awards and notoriety, I went back into this thing the very next year very hesitantly (*because of cost, time, people, etc.*), but decided last minute that if I did it a little differently it would be okay and work... That's where I made the mistakes. *Mistake #1:* I partnered with a deal site to increase exposure, demand and early ticket sales. (*Didn't need to this and never should have done this. Too many people found out too quickly and it was a problem because true quality never goes on sale... I was entertaining people that didn't understand value because I didn't give them a reason to respect me or my brand. Side Note: when was the last time Rolls Royce had a sale? I'm just saying... Things cost what they cost. Not negating favor or a deal, but going on sale is different. A sale is a public announcement that says I can't fully support my current asking price because I don't fully believe in the product I'm selling.)* Mistake #2: I changed venues. *(There is something about creating on a blank canvas that really brings a vision to life. Being in another space that you are renting where you don't have your own identity is detrimental. This is true in business and in life.)* Mistake #3: I rushed this job. *(Remember last minute... Because I had been down this road before I was able to move faster because I had some things already in place, but the reality is that this time around I didn't sit with this project like I did previously. I took my customers for granted and in a sense didn't think or fully focus on their experience. I cut corners and it showed... to me.)* The end result was that I had a function that had the wrong people present and way too many of them. *(Specifically, it was their attitude towards things of high value. I don't blame them because I opened up that can of worms when I discounted a highly valuable product.)* Lastly, the venue was just too small for the level of execution and overall it wasn't great. Now in truth, some people absolutely loved what we did, but I was not feeling the outcome because I focus on the experience. To me, Good is not Great and if it isn't amazing and memorable, I honestly don't want to be a part of it. *(Definition of average is the best of the worst and the worst of the best. I care about people and their experiences. I think that they should be wowed at every opportunity.)*

So that brings us to today… Honest Moment: for the past three years I have been on a self-imposed hiatus. In one sense I needed to reconnect to the things that caused success in the first place, but I also needed to correct course and let the low-value life forces find something else to do. During this time, I found multiple things that was anything and everything except for going back into the arena that I once conquered. It honestly became easy to avoid the fear of what I considered a failure and/or another misdirected execution. The bigger problem was that I was putting 'my' identity in what 'other' people thought of me and how I was letting a simple mistake(s) define me. This in itself is very dangerous because when they like you, you're feeling great. But when you perceive they don't, you can be being depressed or just beating yourself up.

(Never give other people the opportunity to rent space in your mind without your permission... They didn't create you, so they are not the ones that you should spend your time trying to please.)

But a funny thing happened this weekend over a shared story about an amazing machine known as a VitaMix. *(For those that don't know VitaMix is one of the most amazing kitchen gadgets around. I've been told it can create pure concrete by just pulverizing rocks. This is the brand of blender that Smoothie King and all other major smoothie shops use. The reason why your smoothie at home doesn't have the same consistency as Smoothie King... is because you don't have a VitaMix.)* During the VitaMix conversation, I remembered that this same blender was mentioned by one of the chefs in his interview that we conducted as a part of the introduction to the first food rave. So I told my buddy I'd send him the clip and we'd have a cool reference point and chuckle. When I went to send the clip I reviewed it and I was frozen in time. What I saw when I watched it was my passion for what I really do all return. That one clip was a representation of the precision that I had once known. The part of me that I had forgotten and somewhat put aside. It was a part of my dream and was in full digital display *(HD, I might add...)*. And it was in this moment that I realized that I was letting a 3-year-old mistake/failure/good, but not great decision hold me back from attacking and conquering things today. I had to be reminded of my victories that I already had.

It's like the story of David. Before he slayed Goliath, people said he was too small and that this giant was too big. But David said, "When I was protecting the sheep, both a bear and lion came and I killed them with my bare hands. Who is this uncircumcised Philistine that defies the armies of the living God?" The boldness in this response speaks to my soul! *(Some people call the Bible a fantastic fairy tale, and even if you see it that way... these stories are on some next level executions. These 'characters' were no punks.)* The key component in this is that David had to "Replay his Victory". He already knew he had success in this battle before it ever started because he remembered what he had already been through.

So maybe you may be stuck like I was... on hiatus from going after that dream job, dream wife and/or dream life. And if that is the case... I say to you, "Replay Your Victory!" Think about all the things that you have already conquered and realize that this current setback is nothing more than a setup. I challenge you *(You don't need an Ice Bucket for this one...)* to live your dream and "Replay Your Victory!" Each and every one of us has a story of triumph! Pull them out and let's win again and again and again. And get ready... I have some experiences that are on the way!

ONE WORD...

I am reflective of the fact that one word can change your entire outlook on life. Sometimes you stumble upon it as a revelation while reading and then other times a friend is there to say something that helps repair a disconnection. The main thing is that one word can change everything. What we do, what we say and how we live is based on words. Words create our very understanding of life itself. Words are the intangible sensors that define and determine your everyday life. It's amazing at how they make you feel: Happy, Sad, Determined, etc.

Words are vital to our survival and come as an offensive and defensive mechanism for our very own success. As we move throughout today and begin to close out this book, focus on the words around you and see how they shape the world you are a part of. If there is one word that I am focused on today, it is: Grace. Grace is so much more than a word... it is life. And in true fashion, for me... it is something that has changed everything.

THE GLOW...

Like Uncle Ben told Peter Parker... With great power comes great responsibility. Many times we want the power, but are ill-equipped to handle the proper responsibilities. Everything you need to succeed in life has already been provided. It's not that you don't have the power, you just haven't appropriated it properly. Look at what you can do today to prepare you for tomorrow. And if you have ever experienced the cinematic masterpiece of Berry Gordy's 'The Last Dragon' then you already understand "The Glow" ...for it truly is the power of elevation.

DON'T FORGET ABOUT PEOPLE...

I do hope at some point we all will finally realize that "People before Product Yields Profit on Your Projects." We cannot be so concerned with a sale by any means necessary because at some point that 'necessary' will be necessary and when we forget about people... in a sense we really forget about ourselves because the entire reason for us being in business and making an exchange in the first place was to be a solution and solve the problem of someone else.

TAKE. OVER.

* <u>A Special Note:</u> If you have found this book to be informative, enlightening, humorous & engaging... Let me know! My various contact information has been provided in the 'About the Author' section and I look forward to learn of your experience. Also, please share your recommendation of this title with your colleagues, friends and social networks.

Thank You.
-Tony Rouse

Fun Fact: Did you notice that there is no printed text on the back cover of this book?!? I was inspired by billionaire hotelier, Steve Wynn, who when he created his namesake hotel Wynn Las Vegas, chose not put the 'show' on the outside of the venue like in his previous hotel ventures Bellagio and Treasure Island. So the reason this 'book has no back' is because I decided to house the information and adventure inside as opposed to presenting a full display merely for people passing by. In other words... Thank you for reading.

ABOUT THE AUTHOR

Tony Rouse is a Brand Strategy Specialist known as The Curator of High-End Experiences whose revolutionary concepts and projects have achieved international exposure and acclaim. He is a Myers-Briggs hybrid of "The Executive" (ENTJ) and "The Giver" (ENFJ) who created and defined the term, Fully Integrated Lifestyle Marketing (F.I.L.M.) which, as he sees it, takes an unconventional approach to traditional advertising by seamlessly creating experiences for brands in the lives of their target consumers and as such, has become the signature of his award-winning style. Having worked with over 25 Fortune 500 companies in the varied capacities of advisement, representation and consultation, he has also been an emcee on national tours for both NASCAR and Universal Records. By the age of 18, he was a featured performer at Carnegie Hall and today serves as a guest contributor for The Wall Street Business Network. Coupled with a healthy dose of witty wisdom and humorous understanding of the rapidly changing state of consumer affairs, taste, preferences and selection, he effortlessly relates to a world inundated with ever-evolving technology.

For More Information: www.MeetTonyRouse.com
Facebook/Instagram/Twitter: @MeetTonyRouse
Email: SayHello@MeetTonyRouse.com

Additional Titles by Tony Rouse:

Dare 2 D.R.E.A.M.:
The Basics of Building a Brand
(whether it be a person, product or project…)

My Life as a Thought…
A Journey of Grace, Growth & God

Presentation Pep Talk:
The 20-Minute Quick Fix